Where do the Eskimos live?

'Eskimo' is the name that Europeans used. Most Eskimos call themselves *Inuit*, which means 'the people'.

The Eskimos live all over the A[rctic] including Greenland, and the [...] area, and there are lots of diffe[rent...] many different ways of life.

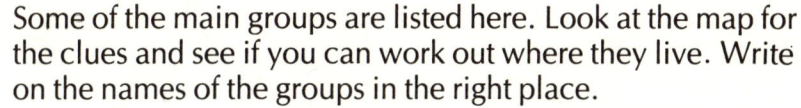

Some of the main groups are listed here. Look at the map for the clues and see if you can work out where they live. Write on the names of the groups in the right place.

The **Aleuts** were employed by the Russians to hunt sea otters.

The **Yupik Eskimo** live in Russia and America, and hunt from boats called *umiaks*.

The **North Alaska Eskimo** are great hunters of the bowhead whale.

The **Caribou Eskimo** live by hunting caribou.

The **Mackenzie Eskimo** travel in very well-built sleds.

The **Netsilik Eskimo** sometimes used polar bear skins as toboggans.

The **Copper Eskimo** used locally found copper to make tools.

The **Polar Eskimo** used iron from a meteorite to make knives.

The **West Greenland Eskimo** defeated the norsemen, the first Europeans in America.

The **East Greenland Eskimo** decorate wooden objects with seals carved from ivory.

The **Ungava Eskimo** sold fox skins to the Hudson's Bay Company from the 1790s.

Animals of the Arctic

This page shows some of the animals that live in the Arctic some or all of the year. All of them are hunted by Eskimos for food and for their skins.

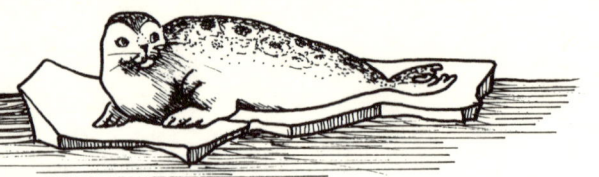

The **seal** is most important creature for the Eskimos. Some kinds of seal can be hunted all year round, and provide food, skins for clothing, fat, sinews for thread, and bones for tools.

The **walrus** is much larger than the seal. It lives in the Arctic all year. Its two long tusks provide ivory for tools and ornaments.

Whales are huge sea-mammals. They come to the Arctic in the summer to feed. One whale provides a lot of food, blubber for lamps, and bones for house beams and tools.

The **polar bear** might travel hundreds of miles across the ice hunting for food. Its white fur is sometimes used for clothes. It takes much skill and courage to hunt the polar bear.

The **Arctic fox** lives in the Arctic all year. In the winter its fur turns white, like the snow. Its white winter coat is used for decorating clothes, and warm trim round hoods.

The **caribou** travels north in great herds in the summer to graze on the tundra. Every winter the caribou hunt takes place and many animals are killed for their skins and meat.

The **musk ox** has a great shaggy coat to protect it against the cold; musk oxen live on the tundra all year round.

Here is a scene on the tundra — the rocky treeless land bordering the Arctic Ocean. In winter it is covered in snow and ice; for part of the time it is dark all day as the sun never rises. In the summer when the snow has melted the flowers bloom and the birds return. For part of the summer the sun never sets and it is light even at midnight.

Finish off this picture. First decide whether it is summer or winter, then draw in the animals that belong there.

Colour your picture in.

Birds

The eider is one of the most colourful birds to visit the Arctic. Some live there all the year round.

Use the key to help you to colour in this picture.

1 white
2 very pale pink
3 grey
4 black
5 orange
6 green

In the summer lots of different birds migrate to the Arctic. You can see some of them on this page. The Eskimos catch them for meat, and use their skins and feathers for clothing and decoration.

Inuktitut

This is Marcusi. He is talking *Inuktitut*, the Eskimo language. If you read the rest of this page you will be able to understand what Marcusi is saying.

Inuktitut means 'the way an Inuk does things,' or 'just like an Inuk.' You can add *-titut* to any word. If you wanted to say 'the way an English person does things' it would be *Englishtitut*.

Inuktitut is completely different from English. And it has very many words and ideas that we do not have.

Tuttu-siuq-guma-punga

When you have read the column on the right write down what you think these sentences mean.

Nanuq tuttu-siuq-guma-puq.

Tuttu-mik malik-puq Marcusi.

Try to write:

Just like a caribou.
She hunts polar bear.
A polar bear wants to hunt a killer whale.

Now, can you tell what Marcusi is saying at the top of the page?
Answers are on the last page

Inuktitut words are sometimes very long. They are built up by putting small pieces in the middle or at the end of a simple word.

Here are some simple words:

tuttu = caribou (pronounced *tooktoo*)
nanuq = polar bear (pronounced *nanoo* – the 'q' sounds like the 'c' at the beginning of 'cough'!)
arlu = killer whale (pronounced *arloo*)
malik = follow

Here are some *infixes* – they go in the middle of words:

–siuq– = hunt (pronouced *see-ok*)
–guma– = want (pronounced *gooma*)
–ngi– = not (pronounced like the 'ngi' in 'longing')

Here are some *affixes* – they go at the ends of words:

–titut = just like a (pronounced *tea-toot*)
–punga = I (pronounced *poonga*)
–putit = you (pronounced *put-it*)
–puq = he or she (pronounced *pok*)

You can use these words to make up sentences. If you use the affix *–mik* it shows that a word is the object of a sentence. For example:

Marcusi arlu-mik malik-puq. Marcusi follows a killer whale.

Marcusi-mik arlu malik-puq. A killer whale follows Marcusi.

Or you can make up one long word:

Arlu-siuq-guma-ngi-punga. I don't want to hunt killer whale.

You can put whole words in any order you like. Just remember that *affixes* always come after *infixes*, and that *infixes* always come after single words.

Everyday life among the Eskimos

Picture like these decorate lots of Alaskan Eskimo tools. They show scenes of everyday life among the Eskimos – in the house, hunting, fishing, travelling by sled and kayak.

Can you tell what is happening in these scenes? Look for pictures of: a dog sled; caribou; bears; a whale; seals; walruses. Can you see anything that looks like fish drying on a rack; men hunting from a boat; men fishing with a big net; people inside a house?

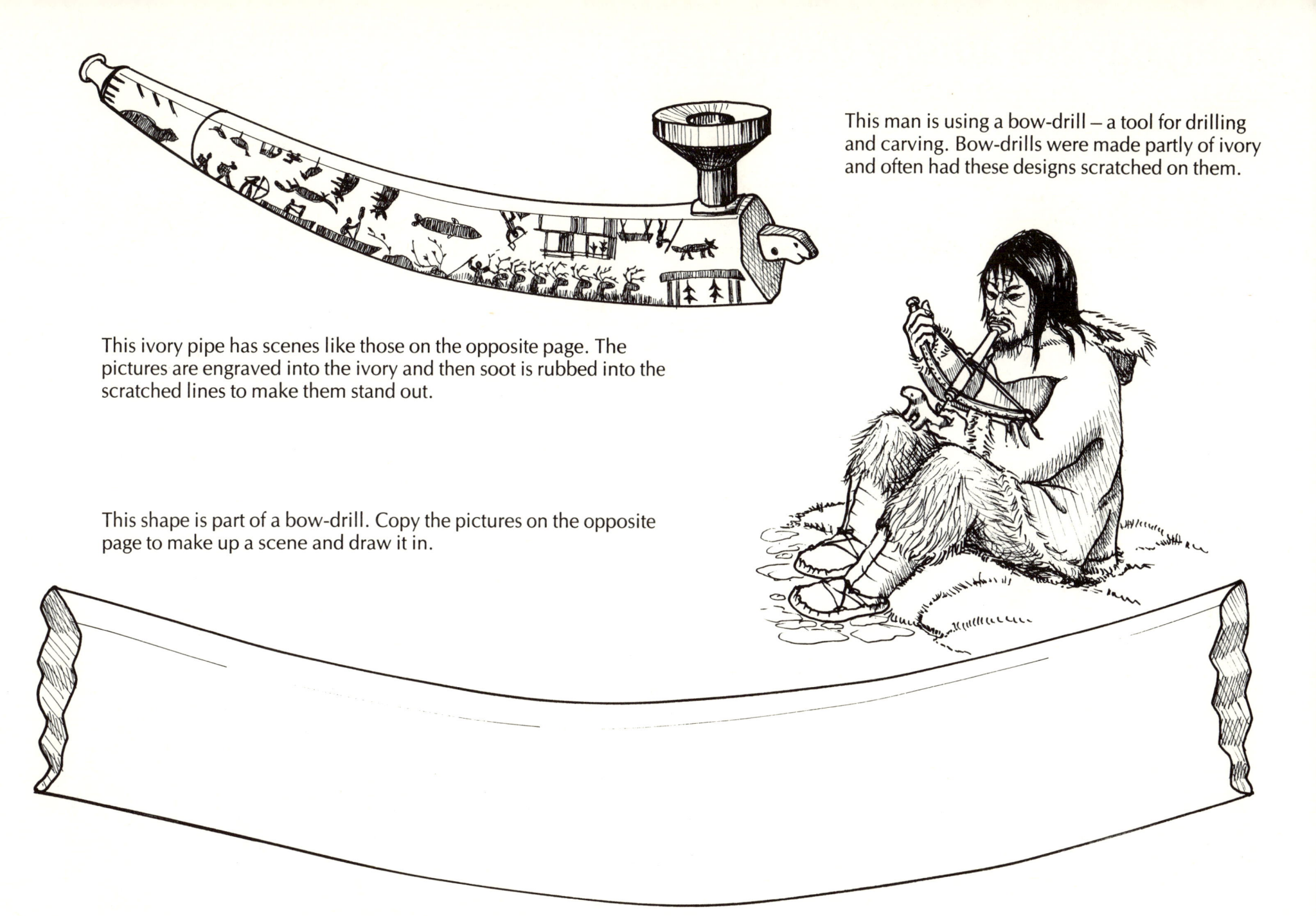

This man is using a bow-drill – a tool for drilling and carving. Bow-drills were made partly of ivory and often had these designs scratched on them.

This ivory pipe has scenes like those on the opposite page. The pictures are engraved into the ivory and then soot is rubbed into the scratched lines to make them stand out.

This shape is part of a bow-drill. Copy the pictures on the opposite page to make up a scene and draw it in.

A paper snow-house to cut out

The Eskimo word for a house is *idlu*. One type of house is built of snow (what we call igloos). They are shaped like a dome, and are made of bricks cut from the snow and built up in a spiral. People moved into them in early winter, and lived in them until the snow began to melt in spring. Nowadays they are used for hunting trips.

Cut out the shapes on this page and stick them together to make your snow-house.

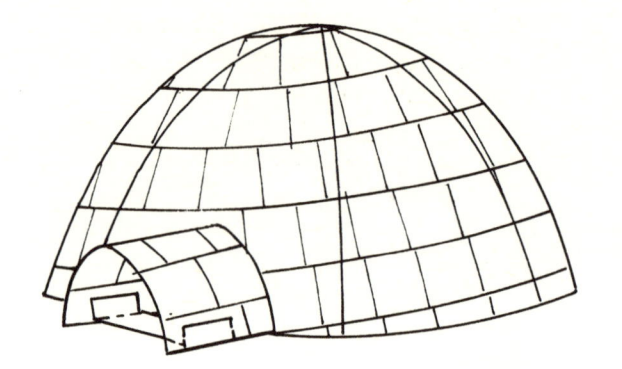

1. Cut out pieces A, B, C, D, E, carefully cutting out the shaded areas between the tabs. Write the letters on the back of each piece as you cut it out, so that you can remember which piece is which.
2. Cut the slits a, b, c, d, e on piece A, and cut out the door.
3. Bend back the tabs on A slightly, glue them and stick them to the underneath of B. Let the glue dry, then stick the tabs of B to the underneath of C, and so on. Make sure that you stick the right pieces together, or the snow bricks will not make a spiral.

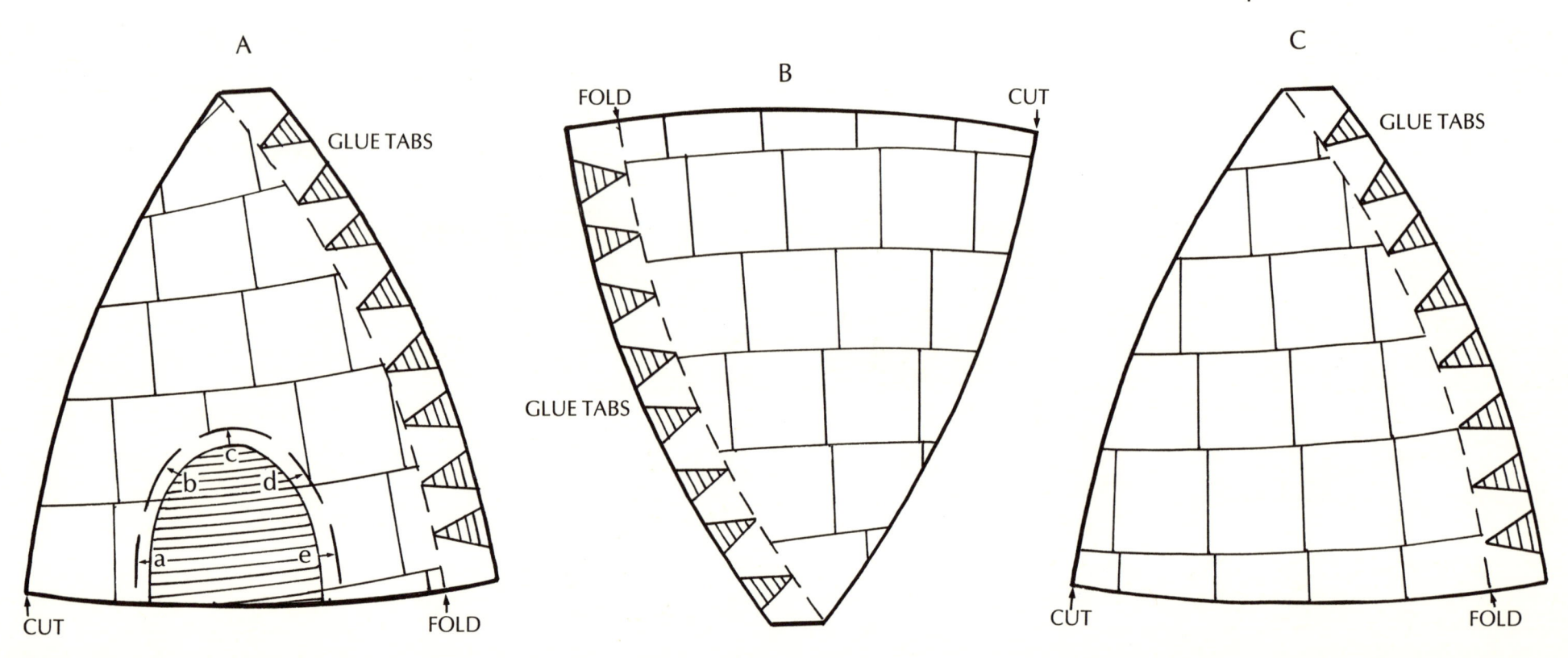

E
FOLD   CUT

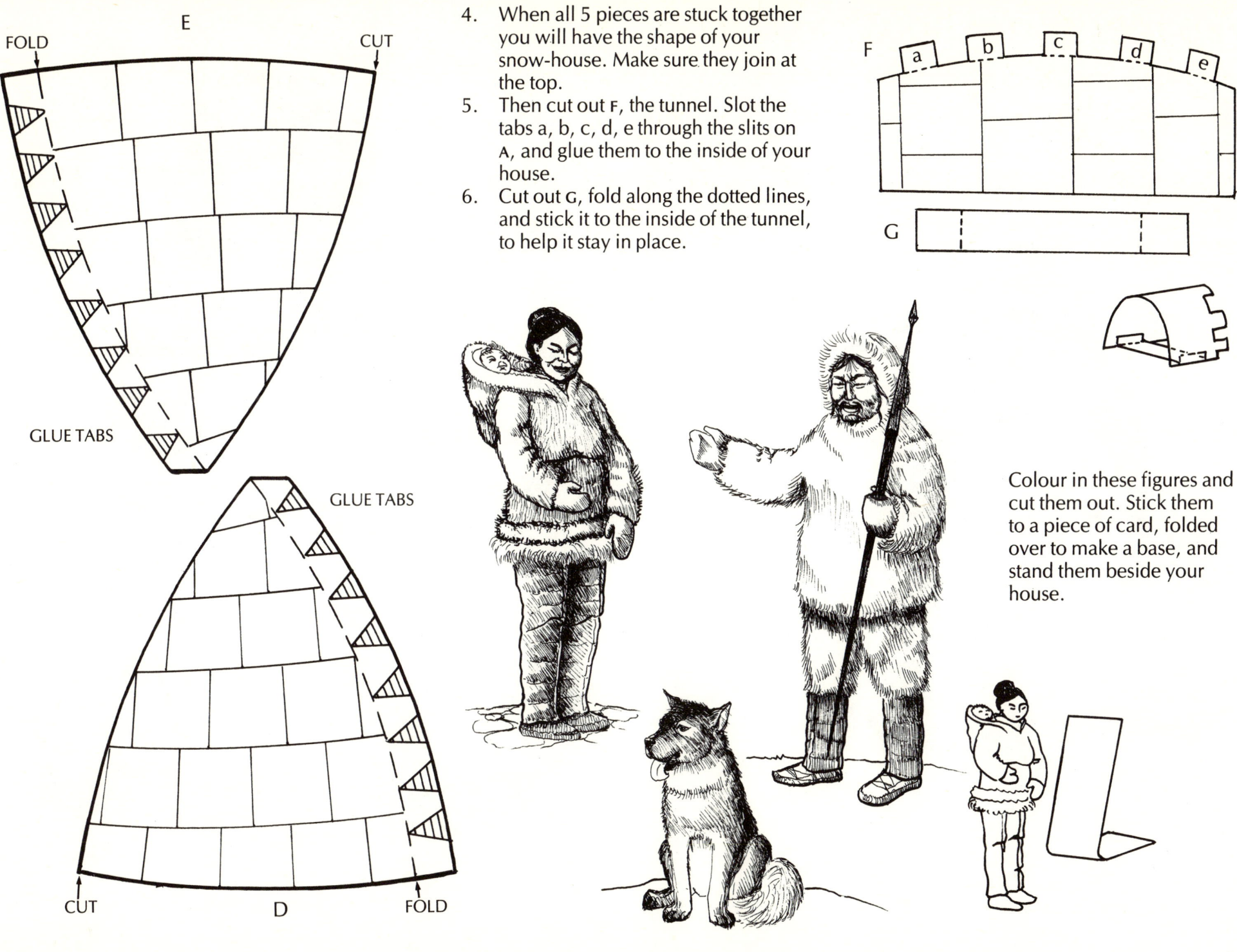

GLUE TABS

GLUE TABS

CUT   D   FOLD

4. When all 5 pieces are stuck together you will have the shape of your snow-house. Make sure they join at the top.
5. Then cut out F, the tunnel. Slot the tabs a, b, c, d, e through the slits on A, and glue them to the inside of your house.
6. Cut out G, fold along the dotted lines, and stick it to the inside of the tunnel, to help it stay in place.

F   a   b   c   d   e

G

Colour in these figures and cut them out. Stick them to a piece of card, folded over to make a base, and stand them beside your house.

9

Tattooing

Some Eskimo women used to decorate their faces with tattoos. When a girl was grown up her face was tattooed by another woman. It was thought to be very beautiful, but it was painful to do. Soot was passed under the skin with the point of a needle to make rows of little dots.

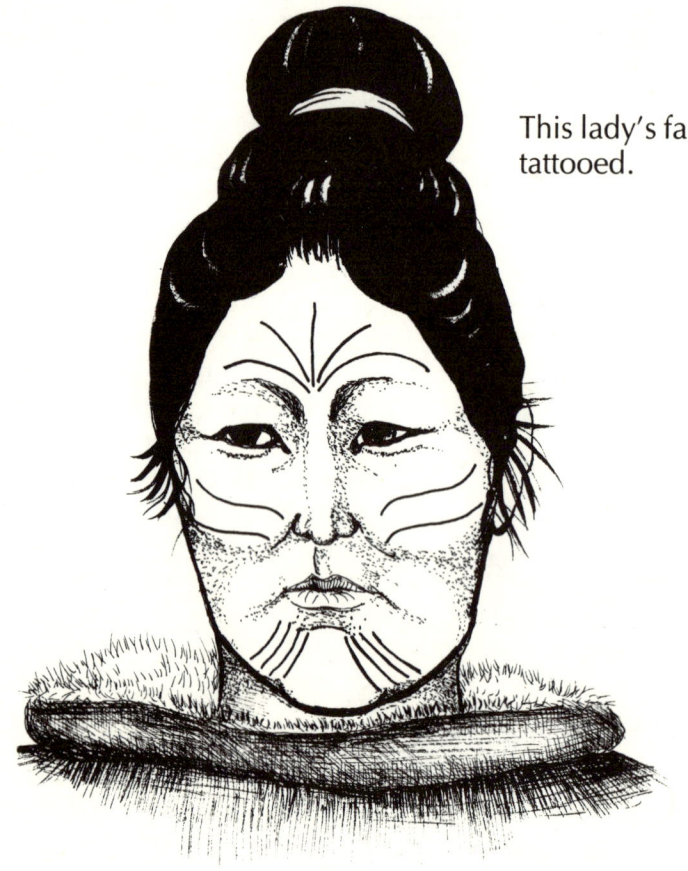

This lady's face has been tattooed.

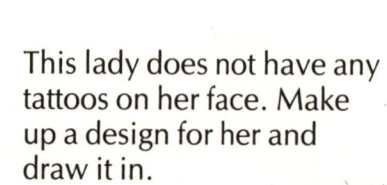

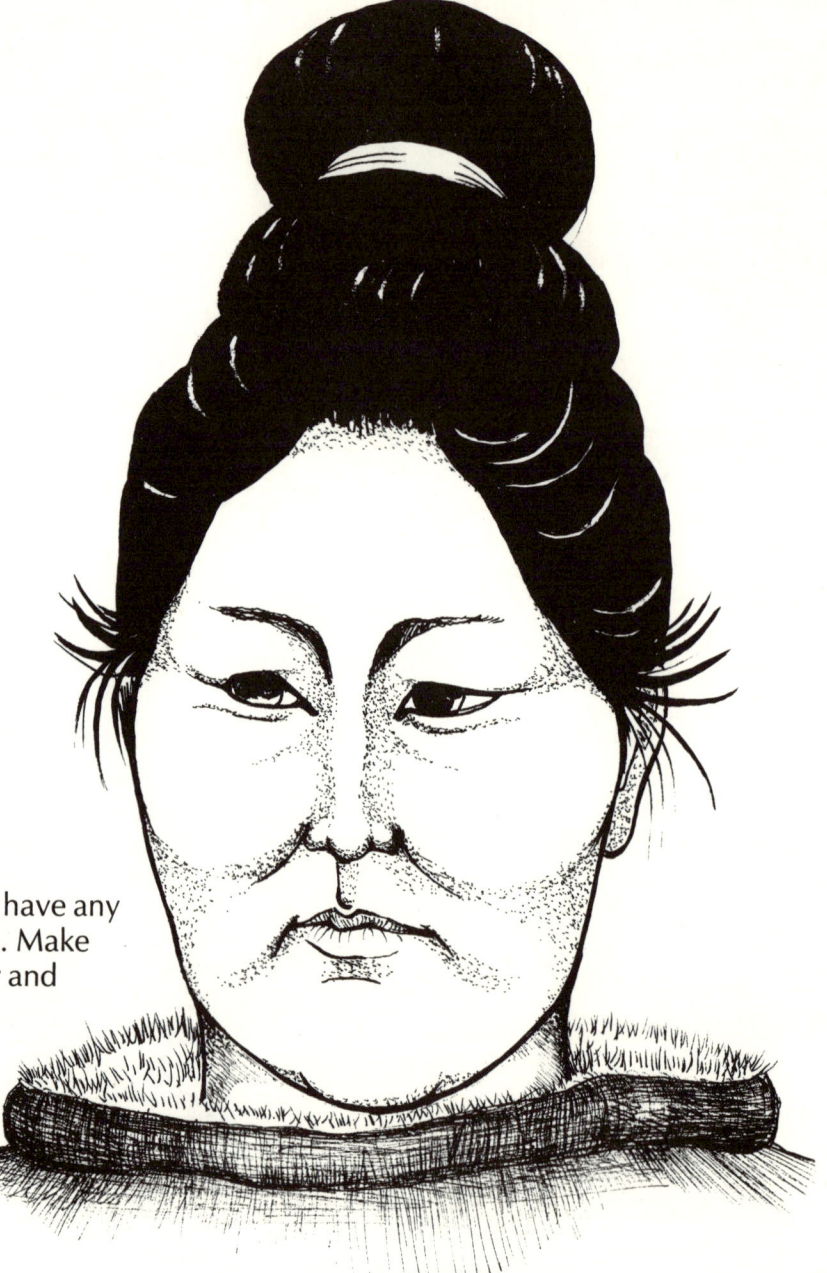

This lady does not have any tattoos on her face. Make up a design for her and draw it in.

Join the dots

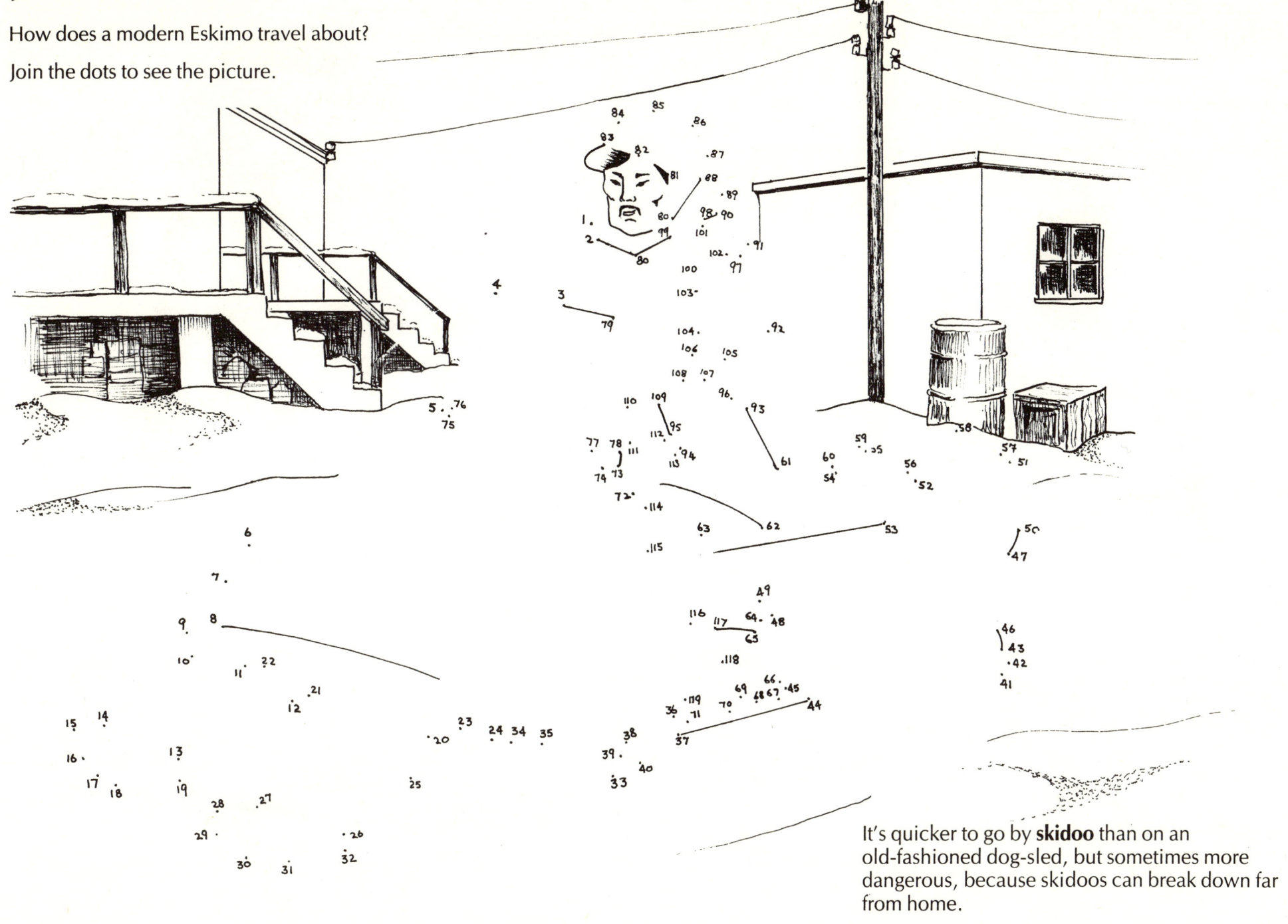

How does a modern Eskimo travel about?

Join the dots to see the picture.

It's quicker to go by **skidoo** than on an old-fashioned dog-sled, but sometimes more dangerous, because skidoos can break down far from home.

Inside an Eskimo house

A picture to colour.

Here is an Eskimo family inside a stone and turf house. The woman is sewing, making clothes; the man is making a harpoon; and the child is playing.

In the old days there wasn't always wood or metal to make things with. What did the Eskimo use instead?

There weren't any trees, but they could get drift wood from the seashore.

They made tools of ivory from walrus and narwhal tusks.

They carved lamps and cooking pots from soapstone which they found on the ground. Now soapstone carvings are sold to the shops.

They used the skins of all sorts of birds and animals.

Every bit of an animal could be used for something. From seals they got:

1. Skins for clothing, tents, kayak covers, and so on
2. Sinews for thread and sewing
3. Oil for cooking and for lamps
4. Meat
5. Bones for tools and so on

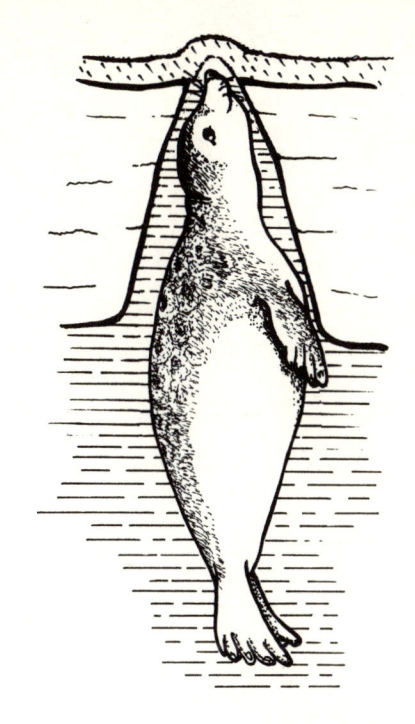

Look at the picture of a Polar Eskimo house on the opposite page and guess what you think they would have used to make:

1. The walls of the house
2. Clothes
3. Needles
4. Cooking pots
5. Lamps
6. Knife
7. The toys
8. The man's harpoon shaft

Answers

1. Slabs of stone covered with turf
2. Animal skins, especially of the seal and polar bear
3. Bone
4. Stone or wood
5. Stone for the base, moss for the wick and oil from blubber
6. Antler and iron
7. Ivory or wood
8. Ivory

Masks

Some Eskimos made masks of animal or human faces. They were used in telling stories and in rituals. They were usually made of wood. Sometimes they were painted, and they also often had feathers, pieces of fur or carved ornaments.

Colour in this mask. You could make a mask of your own. Draw a face on a sheet of card. Colour it in and cut out holes for the eyes, nostrils and mouth. You could also add other decorations – feathers, wool, material and so on. Then cut it out, tie it on with string or elastic and surprise your friends!

Other kinds of masks were finger-masks. They were used by women in dances. The fingers went through the holes at the bottom. These pictures show both sides of one mask. On one side is a bird's head, and on the other a woman's face.

It is easy to make a finger-mask. You could make some of the characters from your favourite story. Draw the mask shape on a piece of card, with a loop at the bottom for the fingers. Paint in the face. Cut the mask out, and add wool for the hair.

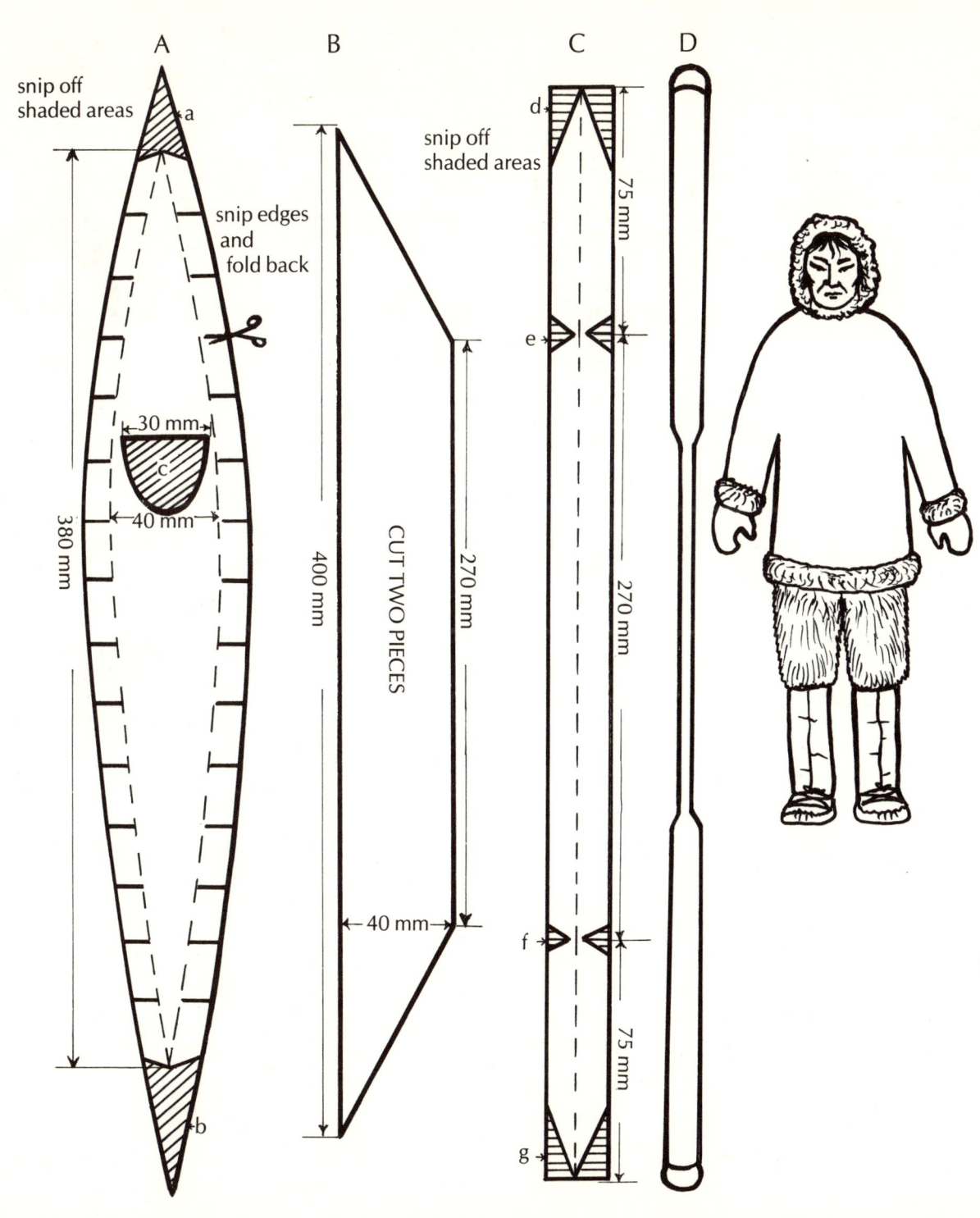

Make a model kayak

1. Copy these shapes onto a sheet of paper, following the measurements carefully. You may find it easier to use graph paper. Remember, you will need two of B.
2. Cut out A, snip off the shaded areas a and b, and cut out c, for the cockpit.
3. Snip the edges of A up to the dotted line and fold under.
4. Cut out B (2 pieces) and stick the long edge to the tabs of A. 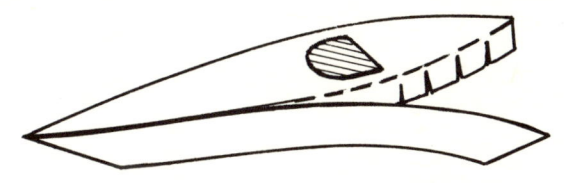
5. Let the joins dry. Then cut out C, fold in half along the dotted line and snip out the shaded areas d, e, f, g. Be careful not to cut it in half!
6. You can now fold C to the same shape as B. 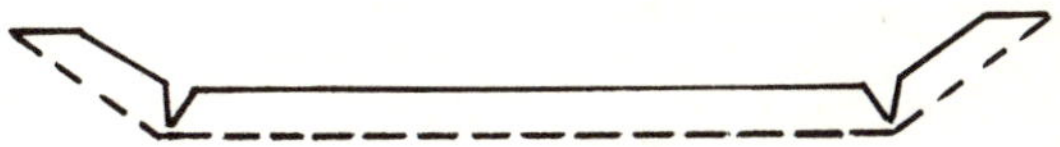
7. Glue C on both sides and stick it on the inside of the edges of B. This holds the two sides together along the bottom edge.
8. Cut out the paddle, D, and stick it to a thin strip of card to stiffen it.
9. Colour your kayak light brown.
10. Now cut out and colour the Eskimo, and fold him so that he sits in the kayak.

Picture Crossword

Complete the crossword by filling in the names of the objects in the right place.

Answers for p. 5

1. *Nanuq tuttu-siuq-guma-puq* = The polar bear wants to hunt caribou.
2. *Tuttu-mik malik-puq Marcusi* = Marcusi follows the caribou.
3. Just like a caribou = *Tuttu-titut*
4. She hunts polar bear = *Nanuq-siuq-puq*.
5. A polar bear wants to hunt a killer whale = *Nanuq arlu-siuq-guma-puq*.
6. Marcusi is saying: 'I want to hunt caribou.'

Drawings by Mary Firman
Devised by J. C. H. King and Jenny Chattington
© 1984 the Trustees of the British Museum
Published by British Museum Publications
46 Bloomsbury Street, London WC1B 3QQ

Reprinted 1985

Typeset by Rowland Phototypesetting Limited,
Bury St Edmunds, Suffolk
and printed in Great Britain by
St Edmundsbury Press,
Bury St Edmunds, Suffolk.